Your Li

30 Days of Joy

Jon Edward Fugler

FINE CHRISTIAN BOOKS
Fuquay-Varina, NC USA

Table of Contents

Before you start…

Download the free Companion Guide

My Joy Journal

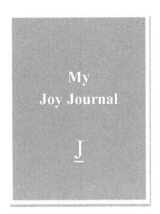

Get the most out of your devotional by keeping a journal as God speaks to you about joy. Key verses from the devotional are included so you can refer to them as you go through this 30-day experience.

You'll also become one of Jon's **VIP Readers**. Receive advance notice of new books in the devotional series **Your Life With God**, as well as inspirational meditations from Jon.

It helps to write things down. Just print out the six pages or use the digital download as a guide for your personal journal.

Visit www.YourLifeWithGod.com/JoyJournal and download your free **My Joy Journal**.

www.YourLifeWithGod.com/JoyJournal

"The joy of the Lord is your strength."

Nehemiah 8:10 (NIV)

Introduction

A couple weeks ago, we had new carpet installed in our home. Everything had to be cleared out of the rooms, which was an ordeal in itself. Move this, move that. Unplug this. Unplug that.

When it came time to put things back and plug things in, I had one brief moment of angst. The computer wouldn't start. This is a big, heavy desktop that we've had for many years. I was beginning to think God was saying, "It's finally time to replace that ancient thing."

After several pushes of the on/off button, wiggling some cords and adjusting the monitor, I finally managed to fire up the beast. My problem was simple. The cord between the computer and the monitor wasn't quite plugged in all the way. It looked like it was plugged in, but in reality, the connection was lost and the screen was black.

The computer was switched on all the time!

Thankfully, that old desktop still has some life in her . . . as long as everything stays connected.

In our own lives, the slightest misconnection with God can kill our joy.

Over the next 30 days, it's my hope that I can help you connect with God in a fresh way so you experience his rich joy consistently.

Joy isn't something you can manufacture. It's a by-product of your relationship with God.

Whether your life is flying along or you're going through tough times, experiencing Jesus' joy will fuel your thoughts, actions, attitudes and words.

I wrote these meditations in a season when my joy was being challenged every day. I needed God's perspective and He filled my soul.

Together, we'll explore how joy intersects with laughter, loss, money, rest, song, shock, betrayal, fellowship and so much more – the normal things of life.

I believe that by spending 30 straight days immersed in this one area, you'll experience God's joy in such a way that it will make a difference for the rest of your life. I encourage you to come back to this devotional whenever you need to be refocused on the quality of joy.

Let's begin the joy journey. I pray that God will change your life as much as He changed mine when I wrote these meditations.

Jon Edward Fugler
Jon@YourLifeWithGod.com

Day 1

Full Joy

"As the Father has loved me, so have I loved you. Abide in my love. If you keep my commandments, you will abide in my love, just as I have kept my Father's commandments and abide in his love. These things I have spoken to you, that my joy may be in you, and that your joy may be full." (John 15:9-11 NIV)

I can't think of any greater, purer, more complete joy we can experience than the joy of Jesus himself. He describes this joy as "full."

Don't you want that? Of course you do.

Why in the world would we try "joy substitutes" when the real thing is already planted inside us if we know Jesus?

My joy substitutes range anywhere from financial security to a Dodger victory. I've got several others, too, if I really take inventory.

How about you? Where does your joy come from?

The correct answer is "Jesus," but don't give that answer unless it's true for you.

We let joy "substitutes" crowd out our Savior. That's why we go from one to another. They don't satisfy for long.

". . . that my joy may be *in you*, and that your joy may be full."

When I hear Jesus saying that to me, I picture joy as a seed waiting to grow. Jesus' joy is inside me, but it only grows when nourished.

What makes it grow? Abiding in Jesus' love.

For the past year, I've begun almost every day by camping on one certain verse. It's familiar to you, I'm sure: "Love the LORD your God with all your heart and with all your soul and with all your strength." (Deuteronomy 6:5 NIV)

I remind myself that loving God is the most important thing I can do. I should find myself evaluating everything I do in light of whether I'm loving God by doing it.

Loving God takes effort. All my heart, soul and strength!

This love relationship with God isn't just one way. Jesus died on the cross out of a deep, deep love for me. God gave his only son because he loved the world so much.

The nourishment for joy to grow in our lives is Jesus' love for us. This kind of love is rich soil, water and sunlight all rolled into one. Just as a seed and plant draw on these elements to grow, we need to draw on Christ's love for our joy to grow.

"that my joy may be in you, and that your joy may be full."

Isn't that wonderful? I can't think of anything more joyful than experiencing the love of God. I'm ecstatic about it when I really consider it. His love produces joy in our lives.

Take a look at that growing thing inside you called "joy." What is it today? A seed? A seedling? A young plant? A thriving tree?

In the quietness of this moment, think about God's love for you. The secret to full joy is abiding in the love of God.

Day 2

Greater Joy

"You have put more joy in my heart than they have when their grain and wine abound." (Psalm 4:7 ESV)

A neighbor drives home with a new car. A friend gets a raise. Your co-worker lands a better job.

However, your life hasn't changed much lately. No new car, raise or high-status job. Life is continuing the same way it did last week . . . last month . . . last year.

You know you should be happy for them, and maybe you are. But, at the same time, are feelings of jealousy creeping in?

Our lives are filled with stuff. So much stuff that storage units seem like the fastest growing business around. Three-car garages are popular, not because we have three cars, but because we need one slot to store all our stuff.

In this verse, the Psalmist is speaking about stuff. Material wealth. He looks around him at all his neighbors' overflowing blessing.

And his response?

Contentment. Joy. In fact, more joy than his neighbors are experiencing with their fabulous blessings.

He speaks to God directly, saying, "You have filled my heart with **greater** joy."

Our joy from the Father is not tied to what we have. Sure, we can be happy and content with wealth and possessions. However, when those go away, does our joy go with them?

If so, that's a sign that our joy isn't God-centric. It's stuff-centric. And maybe it's not really joy at all.

If you can look at your neighbors' material blessings and be rich with joy, your heart is in the right place. According to the Psalmist, that's a good test.

Take time right now and ask God to *fill* your heart with joy. *His* joy. It's not something that you can create on your own. Meditate on the verses surrounding verse 7 from David's Psalm. Pray through them and consider the deep joy that comes only from your relationship with God.

"Be angry, and do not sin;
    ponder in your own hearts on your beds, and be silent.
Offer right sacrifices,
    and put your trust in the LORD.

There are many who say, 'Who will show us some good?
    Lift up the light of your face upon us, O LORD!'
You have put more joy in my heart
    than they have when their grain and wine abound.

In peace I will both lie down and sleep;
    for you alone, O LORD, make me dwell in safety."

(Psalm 4:4-7 ESV)

Day 3

Interrupted Joy

Jackie was cruising through her morning. Her spirits were up. She was accomplishing exactly what she had planned.

It was a good day.

Until her boss stopped by. A single, cutting remark brought her spirits – and her day – crashing down.

With tears welling up, she hung her head low over her desk. It was embarrassing. Her boss was critical. Besides, the remark wasn't true.

A thousand miles away, in his office, Jim was making last-minute preparations for a big meeting. He had a couple seconds, so he decided to check his email.

Mistake.

There sat a message from his boss. And it wasn't good. In fact, the news was so bad that Jim's attention shifted entirely away from his upcoming meeting. His emotions were rattled. His day quickly collapsed.

What do Jackie and Jim have in common? For both of them, they were working in a spirit of joy when, suddenly, they were wounded by someone's words.

I call this "interrupted joy." It came out of nowhere.

There's a good chance you'll face someone or some*thing* that will interrupt your joy today. How you handle it will determine how you feel on the other side of that interruption. It will be a test of the depth of your walk with God.

The key is to be prepared before the surprise hits.

I think you'd agree that our joy shouldn't be dependent upon our circumstances. In reality, though, it's hard to live that way.

You can prepare for interrupted joy. Can I suggest a great practice someone recently taught me?

Think of a trigger word that points you to Jesus when your joy is interrupted. For instance, mine might be "beatitudes." This reminds me of Jesus' Sermon on the Mount. My mind instantly goes there and considers the words Jesus spoke.

"Blessed are the poor in spirit . . . blessed are the merciful . . . blessed are the pure in heart." (Matthew 5:3,7,8 NIV)

I can have the passage memorized or carry it with me on an index card. Better yet, I can have it ready on my phone.

I find that as I go directly to God's Word, I rebound from the surprises and shocks. My joy returns more quickly. Sure, I may not bounce back in an instant, but I do recover.

God's Word has a way of giving us his view on things. We gain an eternal mindset. Once we acquire God's thoughts, the thing that upsets us doesn't have such an impact.

What will your trigger word be today? Where will it take you into *his* Word to keep that joy flowing?

Day 4

EnJOYment

Do you remember the great Vince Lombardi, the Green Bay Packers' Super Bowl champion coach? He was a harsh, ornery guy. He was so strict that if you showed up 10 minutes early for a team meeting, you were really five minutes late! And boy, did he let you have it.

I have all my clocks, as well as my watch, set five minutes early. I love it. It allows me time to relax as I get to where I'm going on time, except to Coach Lombardi's team meetings (which I never attended).

In this crazy, fast-paced world, how often do you stop and enjoy the gifts God has given you?

"Every good gift and every perfect gift is from above, coming down from the Father of lights, with whom there is no variation or shadow due to change." (James 1:17 ESV)

Oh, how we toil, scratch and scrape our way through the day. We hurry. We rush. We beat the clock so we won't be late for school, work, meetings, church, games . . . just about everything.

We can hardly enjoy life at this pace.

Look what's in the center of "enjoyment." Take a good look.

Joy!

EnJOYment.

Shouldn't we enJOY work? We spend most of our lives there!

How about our kids? Shouldn't family bring enJOYment to our lives?

Even our hobbies. Certainly there should be some enJOYment in those.

Enjoy the good gifts God has given you. In fact, today, pick one and really knock yourself out.

Take a kid out on a date. Have a family game night and laugh together. Go to the beach or a park. Read a great book. Call a friend and get caught up for an hour.

These good gifts from God are for your enJOYment. And enJOYment is good.

Let me warn you. To truly enjoy one of these good gifts from God above, you'll have to make time. That means saying "no" to something to make room for God's good gift.

It could mean getting up early to take care of time-snatchers. Or staying up late to get a task done.

Our Lord Jesus Christ is the only source for the deepest, longest lasting joy. No doubt about that. But enjoy his gifts, too.

If you make a practice of enJOYing every good and every perfect gift from above, you'll experience a richness of joy that you may be missing.

What's your starting point today?

Day 5

Feeding Your Joy

Have you ever met someone who is constantly happy, smiling, laughing, looking on the bright side — always? You'd think this person would bring joy to our lives, but they often annoy us.

It could be that they aren't joyful at all, even though they appear to be.

Joy is not a constant emotional high. Yet, we expect it to be. We beat ourselves up when joy seems to leave us. We whisper to ourselves that we aren't living up to God's standards because we aren't joyful.

Joy is deeper than an emotional high. The roots of joy run to our soul, just like a flourishing tree has roots running deep underground. Sometimes joy is expressed in peace, contentment, assurance, faith or a relaxed spirit.

Joy has to be fed. Where do you turn to feed your joy?

I can easily turn to the things of this world to try to feed mine. It doesn't last long, because my soul has an insatiable appetite that temporal things can't satisfy.

God's Word feeds our joy. Not a surface reading, but an immersion into his Holy Book. And that takes time.

Immerse yourself into one of these passages of Scripture today, then the others in the days ahead. These truths will feed your soul.

- Philippians 4:4-8. This passage starts with, "Rejoice in the Lord always. I will say it again: Rejoice!" (NIV) In these five verses, you'll find encouragement. You'll also receive instruction on how to keep godly thoughts on the forefront of your mind. These thoughts will fill your soul and bring joy.

- Luke 24. The resurrection of Jesus. This is a detailed account of his appearance to many and their reactions. Luke writes in a way that draws you into the story and makes you feel like you are right there with him and the others.

- John 14:1-4. Jesus promises his disciples that he is going to prepare a place for them in heaven. The same is true for us. Read this and let your mind focus on the eternal, rather than the temporal here on earth. Your heart will be lifted up as you meditate on these verses.

You may want to approach the passage in this way:

1. Read the passage.

2. Silently think about it and see what God brings to your mind.

3. Read it aloud a few times.

4. Pray whatever comes to mind in response to God's Word.

This practice should never become a ritual. It's a great way to slow down and let the Word penetrate your heart. Feed your joy.

Day 6

Joy and a Day Away With God I

One of the richest spiritual experiences I enjoy is taking a day away with God. I've heard others say the same thing.

There's something special that happens when I have unrushed, often unstructured, time with God. I push away my regular activities and responsibilities to be with Jesus. It's that simple. Yet, profound at the same time.

While I experience tremendous benefits from my day away with God, it's not really about me. The day with Him is a time of fellowship and communion at a level that can't happen any other way. My day away with God is really about Him. And I receive so many benefits.

Sometimes I start by praying. Other times I begin by camping on a passage from Scripture. Or I might turn up praise music to get started. There are times I have more structure to my day. But I have one rule . . . there are *no* rules!

Let me tell you about my day away with God last week. Soon after I woke up, He brought these words to my mind. You may recognize them:

"Blessed assurance, Jesus is mine. Oh what a foretaste of glory divine. Heir of salvation, purchase of God, born of his Spirit, washed in his blood."

The words kept running through my mind. They centered my whole being on Jesus. I started singing the words. For two or three hours, I was lost in them and in the entire song. I have to tell you, I was having my own little joy party.

By the time I reached the chorus of that great hymn, I was all smiles and singing loud, "This is my story, this is my song, praising my Savior all the day long . . . this is my story, this is my song, praising my Savior all the day long!"

If, at this moment, you're thinking, "Yes, I need this!" then that's God drawing you to himself. He desires the time with you. He loves you.

However, it may be impossible to carve out a full day to be with Jesus.

Your life may revolve around young children or even a new baby in the home. Your job may be so demanding you can't take time off any time soon. You might even be working two jobs and barely have enough time to eat and sleep. You're exhausted! Or it could be that you and God aren't getting along that well right now.

If any of those situations describes your life, then you need a day away with God more than ever. Obstacles like this are Satan's way of keeping you from God. You'll end up spiraling down further and further emotionally, physically and spiritually.

The pace of life can overwhelm you and you need a Sabbath rest. A day away with God is a time of restoration.

The most important thing you can do at this moment is to say, "Yes, I will carve out time to get away with God to restore my soul."

Let's not consider the "how" just yet. For now, merely say, "Yes." We'll deal with the how tomorrow. I'll show you what you can do to make your retreat with God a reality, and what to do once you get there.

Thank you for stepping out boldly. It will change your life and bring a depth of joy you may not have experienced in a long time.

Day 7

Joy and a Day Away With God II

So you've said "Yes!" you'll have a day away with God. Congratulations! This could be the most important decision you'll make for your spiritual health.

When it comes to experiencing consistent joy, I can't think of a better foundation to lay. It's not the mechanics of a day away with God that make the difference. It's the fact that you'll be **with** God for a day, enjoying fellowship with Him.

"Life **with** God is different because its goal is not to **use** God, its goal **is** God." (Skye Jethani, *With*)

Today, we're going to dive into "how." How do you make this day happen? How can you experience rich, undistracted fellowship with God?

First of all, to put you at ease, let me say that there is nothing magical about a full day. If you can only set aside a half day, do it! If you have to get up in the middle of the night and begin at 3 am before work, that's ok. While a full day is not the only method, anything less than four hours will make it difficult to really settle in and quiet your heart before the Lord. You need uninterrupted time to enjoy deep fellowship.

Here are three suggestions for how you can make the most of your day with God. While structure is not necessary, you may find structure helpful for you to stay focused.

1. **The Lord's Prayer.** A friend of mine, Steve Harling, often uses the Lord's Prayer to guide him through the first part of the day. He starts with, "Our Father in Heaven,

hallowed be your Name." Steve explains that Scripture reminds us that the Lord inhabits the praises of his people. "Experience the presence of the Lord," says Steve. "Engage your heart and mind in worshiping him." He suggests that you compose an A-to-Z list of your Heavenly Father's attributes or characteristics.

2. **Listen to praise and worship music**. Whether it's modern praise or classic hymns, either is a great way to let your spirit be enveloped in praise. Pandora is the perfect tool for this. There are times when I don't want any lyrics at all, so I listen to the instrumental Christian music channel. Yes, there is one of those. Your mood will dictate the music you hunger for.

   After the time of worship music, spend time in prayer as God leads. Worship him, confess any sin, turn over your burdens to him, bring needs to God, enjoy your sweet fellowship with him. Let your spirit relax in his presence. And . . . listen.

3. **Engage with Scripture.** I remember walking down a trail one day a couple months ago, memorizing a passage of Scripture. I spent most of two or three hours on it as I walked, reading it aloud and saying it forcefully and joyfully. I was so immersed in it that the words came alive for me. I had read the passage many times before, but focusing on each word and phrase brought it to life. The Holy Spirit encouraged and empowered me through that experience. I go back to that passage occasionally for inspiration and truth.

These are three guides you can use to make your day away with God a rich time of refreshment and connection. Now's the time to check your calendar and schedule your day away with God.

Day 8

Joy and Betrayal

Think of a time when you've been betrayed by someone you trusted. There are few things as painful as that.

Emotions flood in. Anger. Grief. Anger. Frustration. Anger.

I know about betrayal. It happened to me not too long ago. And I'm dealing with it. I may have suppressed some of the emotions, but I am sure they will emerge over the next few days.

Here's where I went with it.

I thought about how I had trusted that person with confidential information. Then he broke my trust by sharing it with another person, and it got back to me.

I have three choices. Cut him off, confront him or pretend like nothing ever happened.

Wait. There's a fourth, and I've chosen that one.

I will forgive.

Forgiveness breaks down the walls Satan is trying to put up between people. Especially between believers.

We betray Jesus every day and he forgives us.

"Bear with each other and forgive one another if any of you has a grievance against someone. Forgive as the Lord forgave you." (Colossians 3:13 NIV)

That perspective sheds a whole new light on our situation.

When I made the choice to forgive, peace settled into my heart.

And as the hours go by, I know that joy will return.

You're involved in a spiritual war. Broken trust is part of that war. You need to fight with spiritual weapons. Forgiveness is one of those weapons. It's like putting water on a fire.

Sure, I do have to deal with the relationship directly. As I've thought about how, I've concluded that I need to do it as a godly man and first submit myself to Jesus. Go to that person as Jesus would. I must exercise humility, even though I am the one who was offended.

Is there someone who has betrayed you that you have not yet forgiven? If so, a piece of your joy has been ripped away. To restore it, you'll need to take that courageous step and forgive.

Forgiveness cancels Satan's power. Then you can move on to approach that person with humility. Have an attitude that will bring glory to God.

This is a case where joy won't return instantly. It will take time. You've been wounded.

Healing of your soul and the relationship are necessary for joy to have its full effect in your heart.

"Then Peter came up and said to him, 'Lord, how often will my brother sin against me, and I forgive him? As many as seven times?' Jesus said to him, 'I do not say to you seven times, but seventy times seven.'" (Matthew 18:21-22 ESV)

Day 9

Joy and Fellowship

Isolation is one of the most painful conditions a person can be in. I heard a speaker tell the stories of the persecuted believers in one particular country. He reported that the imprisoned believers were beaten, ridiculed and tortured for their faith. However, it was not this treatment that caused them the most pain.

It was being kept in solitary confinement, apart from any other believers. That's what really crushed their spirits.

Isn't it ironic that for many Christians in the free world, they choose isolation? Church attendance is an option. They don't spend time with other believers.

Isolation robs us of a main ingredient for joy: fellowship.

The Bible tells us that, "As iron sharpens iron, so one person sharpens another." (Proverbs 27:17 NIV). We need each other.

The late Bill Bright, founder of Cru, would compare fellowship to a fire. One burning log alone will die out quickly, but if you keep adding logs, you have a hot, healthy fire. Imagine the magnitude of a bonfire!

Would you like your joy to flourish? Give attention to fellowship.

It's not enough to merely attend church. The real results come when you commit to other believers on a deeper level.

First-generation Christians modeled it for us: "They devoted themselves to the apostles' teaching and to fellowship, to the breaking of bread and to prayer." (Acts 2:42 NIV)

Engage in one-on-one coffee shop meetings where you include

prayer and studying Scripture together. Invite others into your home for a meal. And small groups are exceptional settings. Use these times as opportunities to be there for each other and pray for each other.

Joy will grow inside your soul. You're not doing the Christian life alone.

If you're already active in your church and/or small group, that's great. Consider what you can do to take that fellowship with believers to a deeper level. Perhaps God is calling you to invest more fully in the lives of others.

You may want to consider finding a prayer partner that you meet with regularly. Find a place where you're not interrupted by other people. This can be the deepest level of fellowship you'll experience as you seek God's face, open up with each other and trust God together.

Just as fire produces more heat when logs are added, your Christian life will experience greater joy when you add the ingredient of deeper fellowship.

Take that step. Depending on where you are in your fellowship journey, consider one or more of these steps:

1. Commit to a local body of believers. Perhaps you're on the fringes of your church or not involved in a church at all. Change that.
2. Actively seek out a small group in your church that you can join. Or start one!
3. Name three to five people with whom you can go deeper as a prayer partner. Then ask them, one at a time, until someone says "yes."

Day 10

Joy and Laughter

They say that laughter has a healing effect on the body. In fact, the Bible tells us, "A cheerful heart is good medicine." (Proverbs 17:22 NIV) Laughter may even release some happy hormones.

In any case, laughter is indeed good for the soul.

When was the last time you had a real hearty laugh? What brought it on? The thought of that memory makes you smile, I'm sure.

I think we all need to set everything aside and laugh. Not just a snicker. But the kind of laugh you just remembered. One that's out of control. Even embarrassing.

Why is it that Christ-followers are often the least happy people in the bunch? We have the living God inside of us. That alone should bring us great joy. And joyful laughter.

Speaker and comedian Ken Davis has a radio feature called "Lighten Up." No matter what the topic that day, he always ends the show with, "Lighten up . . . and live!" You see, Ken has a joyful perspective on life, even when telling tough stories.

So how do we manage to laugh when we're faced with the realities of life that aren't funny at all?

Work challenges don't make you laugh. Family conflicts aren't funny. Health problems are painful. The thought of the destiny of the unsaved isn't laughable.

Yet, because these very things surround us, we need to find time to laugh.

You may need a good laugh right now. You might be in a funk and laughter is the prescribed medicine.

Can I give you permission to laugh today? Will *you* give yourself permission to laugh?

I guarantee that a good laugh will chase away the spirit of bitterness, sadness or anger that you might be feeling right now. Laughter and bitterness can't co-exist. Laughter pushes sadness away. Laughter beats anger every time.

What is it that will bring laughter into your life?

For me, it's crazy comedy. Most anything with Kevin James will make me laugh on the spot. King of Queens reruns, Mall Cop, Kevin Can Wait. (I was bummed when that show was cancelled).

Not real spiritual, is it? That's ok. Yours doesn't have to be either, as long as it doesn't dishonor God.

Laughter is a joy trigger. It takes your mind off the things that rob your joy and opens the door to consider those things that *bring* you joy.

"Whatever is true, whatever is noble, whatever is right, whatever is pure, whatever is lovely, whatever is admirable — if anything is excellent or praiseworthy — think about such things." (Philippians 4:8 NIV)

In Ken's words, "Lighten up and live!"

Consider today…

- What makes you laugh? I mean *really* laugh? Whatever it takes, spend some time diving into one or more of those things as soon as you can today.

- How can you make someone else laugh today? Be one who releases the joy trigger in their life.

Day 11

Joy and Loss

When my mom died at her young age, it was a tough time during a cold December week in Upstate New York. As usual, it was cloudy. Snow was on the ground and it fell almost every day.

The stark, gray environment contributed to the mood that filled the air for my family. We were all pained in a big way by the loss of a wonderful woman who had given herself for us.

I remember how she would squirrel away extra grocery money in one of the drawers. She would send it to me at college to help me out. You can imagine what a $20 bill in the mail meant to a college kid.

I have tears in my eyes as I write these reflections, some 35 years later.

Loss.

How can joy be restored in our lives when we are going through such a time?

When we lose someone close to us, indescribable emotions take over. Whether a loved one's death comes slowly or suddenly, the finality of it all has a profound effect on us.

We reflect on our past with that loved one. We might move back and forth from happiness to sorrow as our mind races through history.

There's no formula for restoring joy in our lives in a season of loss. This isn't a math equation. The ebb and flow of life isn't predictable.

I do know that our Savior's healing touch is an element in restoring joy. Allowing him into our loss and sorrow is critical.

Time is also part of it. Letting those feelings just happen.

Can we move from sorrow to joy instantly? I don't think so. It's a journey.

Joy will gradually return when we gaze at Jesus, spend time with him and allow him to capture our heart and emotions.

The author of Hebrews says we are in the right place when we are fixing our eyes on Jesus, the pioneer and perfecter of faith.

Jesus knows greater pain and sorrow than we are experiencing in our loss. When he went to the cross, he was separated from the Father he had been one with for eternity. He was ripped away from that perfect relationship.

"For the joy set before him he endured the cross, scorning its shame." (Hebrews 12:2 NIV)

He knows your sorrow in your loss. His arms are wide open to comfort you as long as you need. He will restore your joy by speaking the eternal into your soul. Once Jesus went through the pain of separation, he was resurrected "and sat down at the right hand of the throne of God." (Hebrews 12:2 NIV)

You, too, have an eternal home prepared for you with the Father. While the truth of that promise may not sink in right now, let it work into your soul as you sit with Jesus in your season of loss.

Day 12

Joy and Money I

There aren't too many things more powerful than money that will affect a person's joy.

Too much of it can make us miserable.

Too little of it can make us depressed.

Losing money, like in the stock market, can make us panic.

A misbalanced checking account ledger can make us anxious.

Many years ago, my wife and I considered ourselves poor. By the world's standards, we were not. But at the time, we were so strapped for cash — regularly — that we often had to collect our pennies for a then 25-cent Thrifty ice cream cone.

We soon discovered we weren't alone in our situation. Several others in our church felt the same way . . . poor and discouraged. Certainly joy-depleted.

So I decided to call everyone together for a "Poor Man's Prayer Meeting." Yep, that's what I called it. As a result, it turned this discouraging situation into something we could laugh about.

I remember it to this day, decades later. We gathered in our living room. We didn't complain. We didn't moan. We prayed. I don't recall the details of our prayers, but I do remember that evening being a turning point for my wife and me.

No, not because we became rich after that. We didn't. But, God filled our hearts with a confidence in Him. We all left that meeting knowing the God of provision, Jehovah-Jireh, a little bit better.

I believe our increase in confidence also related to the fact that we came together with other believers in the same predicament. We understood each other's struggle. There's strength in that. Not for a pity party, but to be transparent. To pray for each other. To lock arms.

Families in desperate need filled the living room. We sought God together. And it was fun.

By focusing on Jesus, it took our minds off our financial stress. Doing it together amplified our faith in the Lord. As we praised God and laid our needs before him, it was transforming. We left the meeting joyful.

Is the lack of money sapping your joy? Is the day-to-day financial grind occupying your mind all the time?

Call together a "poor man's prayer meeting." Seek God with others who are in the same boat. It could be your turning point. Your joy is likely to return.

Day 13

Joy and Money II

Money can be your enemy or your friend. It can cry out, "Keep me! You need me!" Or "Give me away!"

Of course, money doesn't speak to us. It's dead, inanimate, neutral, neither good nor bad.

We're the ones who speak to ourselves about money. And are we ever convincing.

We know many Bible verses about money. Like these:

"No one can serve two masters. Either he will hate the one and love the other, or he will be devoted to the one and despise the other. You cannot serve both God and money." (Matthew 6:24 NIV)

"Do not wear yourself out to get rich; do not trust your own cleverness. Cast but a glance at riches, and they are gone, for they will surely sprout wings and fly off to the sky like an eagle." (Proverbs 23:4-5 NIV)

Somehow, knowing or even memorizing verses like these doesn't seem to change our heart or our emotions. Committing 2 Corinthians 8:7 to memory doesn't fill our heart with joy.

"But since you excel in everything — in faith, in speech, in knowledge, in complete earnestness and in the love we have kindled in you — see that you also excel in this grace of giving." (NIV)

Do you know what does? *Acting out* 2 Corinthians 8:7.

We need to give our money away. The more we give, the more

joy we'll experience.

Test it out. Start small.

Think of someone you know that could use a little help. What's their name? Help them.

That's it. It's as simple as . . . well . . . giving your money away.

God has created us with the need to give. It's a reflection of our Father himself. He gives and gives and gives every day. We call his gifts "blessings."

He even marked history by giving – his Son Jesus.

God's blessings are large and small. So should our giving be.

I'm sure a person popped into your mind when I asked you to think about someone in need.

Don't let your joy be robbed by ignoring the Holy Spirit's tap on your shoulder. Help that person today.

I guarantee you'll feel joy.

Try it again tomorrow. It's habit-forming. And it's what God wants you to do.

Day 14

Joy and Rest I

The alarm goes off in the morning. The race is on. You crawl out of bed at a turtle's pace and make it to the shower. As you run the upcoming day through your mind, your senses come alive. In fact, your world becomes intense.

Kids to school, Jamie to the dentist appointment, report due today for my boss, meeting where I'm presenting, two after-school practices for soccer in two different places, get dinner done tonight in time for Bobby's lessons . . . just pick up burgers.

It's no wonder that joy has escaped the average Christian. There's no room for it in the schedule.

But the problem is deeper than that. You don't rest. You're chasing life, whether it be a full schedule with kids or activities of your own.

The truth is that anxiety, fear, rushing and striving take the place of joy.

Instead of kicking yourself and being disappointed in your lifestyle, here's a suggestion.

Rest.

Yes. Rest.

"But I don't have time!" you say. "You've just described my life to a *t*.

Not a good excuse. Jesus had one of the most demanding schedules I can think of and he found time to rest. Even in crisis.

"On that day, when evening had come, he said to them, 'Let us go across to the other side.' And leaving the crowd, they took him with them in the boat, just as he was. And other boats were with him. And a great windstorm arose, and the waves were breaking into the boat, so that the boat was already filling. But he was in the stern, asleep on the cushion. And they woke him and said to him, 'Teacher, do you not care that we are perishing?'" (Mark 4:35-38 ESV)

Can you rest when the constant winds and waves of life smack you around?

I think it's time to change your schedule so there's room for rest. You'll have margin in your life to recuperate, refresh and rejuvenate. You must find the time.

Start today and carve out 20 minutes to rest. It may come at lunch, where you simply go to your car and sit there, emptying your heart to the Lord. Or even taking a nap.

Jesus invites you. "Come to me, all you who are weary and burdened, and I will give you rest." (Matthew 11:28 NIV)

Give yourself permission to rest today. And tomorrow. And the next day.

We are finite creatures and we need the replenishing practice of rest. Without feeling guilty for enjoying it.

If you practice rest on a daily basis, I know that the joy of the Christian life will seep back into your life.

Day 15

Joy and Rest II

Yesterday, we discussed the lost practice of rest. I do hope you found 20 minutes to rest. If so, I applaud you. If not, I'll applaud you tomorrow, right?

There's more to rest than taking 20 minutes here and there, but that daily practice will bring more joy to your life. The pressure of your schedule will be buffered by this simple practice.

God made us for more than that, though. It's the reason He created the Sabbath. Our Father knows we have a spiritual, physical and emotional need to take time off. To unplug from the world.

So, today, let's open the possibility of taking an extended time of rest. Instead of minutes or hours, let's consider days.

We should have a rhythm of daily rest, as I challenged you yesterday. Followed by weekly rest, modeled for us by God creating the Sabbath for our benefit. We should have monthly rest in our rhythm of life. And more extended rest during the year as part of our annual rhythm. We call that "vacation."

Rest is hard, isn't it? Has it occurred to you that the pressures of life could be stealing your joy? Our spiritual, emotional and physical health depend on rest. As does our joy!

So here's the deal. I know you have a packed schedule. So do I.

Take out your calendar for the rest of the year and block out rest. Especially a vacation of more than one day. Perhaps a long weekend or, better yet, an entire week. And another one a few months down the road. Log them into your calendar or block them out if you've got a calendar on the wall.

Protect those blocks of rest. Don't let anyone take them away.

A final thought about rest in general. It's different for everyone. And it's not always being still and quiet.

Recreation is rest, because it allows us to escape life's pressures and schedules for a while.

Playing board games is rest for some.

Working out can be rest, believe it or not. It releases those happy hormones into our bodies.

Reading is rest . . . if you like to read.

For me, writing is rest. I dream of extended days of writing on an island in Hawaii. That would be the ultimate rest for me.

Whatever refreshes you is rest.

When you schedule your times of rest, keep in mind that you do not have to be in a monastery environment. The purpose is to unplug, refresh and relax.

At the same time, it is also important for us to slow down regularly and have time alone. Don't miss out on that sweet time of stillness, where you can rest with our God.

"Be still and know that I am God." (Psalm 46:10 NIV)

Day 16

Joy and Sickness

"Consider it pure joy, my brothers and sisters, whenever you face trials of many kinds." (James1:2 NIV)

I'm a wimp when I'm sick. I complain and I want to be left alone.

My wife, on the other hand, never complains. Even during her cancer treatment, she never once complained. She had good reason to, but always remained positive. Even on the hardest days during chemo, and its side-effects, she remained steady.

The past three weeks, I've been living in pain. I've made sure everyone knows it, too. This is a serious condition and I deserve sympathy and recognition.

My pain? I sprained my left index finger and it's not healing fast enough for me.

"How petty," you say. You're right. As I said, I'm a wimp.

How do you handle pain and sickness? Like me or like my wife?

Staying joyful in sickness or pain is not easy. In fact, it's probably impossible -- in our own power. This is a time when you need the Holy Spirit to lift you above circumstances.

Pain and sickness test our depth of joy. If we're experiencing the joy of the Lord, truly experiencing it deep inside, then it will help us when we're down and out.

In other words, train for pain. Don't wait until pain or sickness hit to try to conjure up some joy. Cultivate joy in your relationship with God so you're better equipped when the pain arrives.

Here are some suggestions for your "joy training" today:

Praise God. Praise should be a daily practice that builds an attitude of joy in your life. Choose a few Psalms that are centered on praise. Read them. Read them aloud. Pray them to God. Your heart will be uplifted, which is what the Psalmist experienced.

Imagine an underground river running below the desert. Plants are thriving in the sand above because they have tapped in to the life-giving water below. Praising God each day creates a river of life running below the surface of your heart.

Thank God. "Praise God from whom all blessings flow" is the beginning of a song our family sings when we get together. Even our three-year-old grandson knows it. We need to recount God's blessings instead of letting them pass through our lives unnoticed. Spend a few minutes thanking God, leading with the eternal – salvation, Jesus' sacrifice on the cross, our righteousness in Christ before God and being a child of God.

Paul says it this way, "Blessed be the God and Father of our Lord Jesus Christ, who has blessed us in Christ with every spiritual blessing in the heavenly places." (Ephesians 1:3 ESV)

Ask God. God invites you to approach him about anything. He seeks an intimate relationship with you that has no secrets. No hidden thoughts or desires. No shame. He knows what's on your heart already, so tell him. Ask him anything. When you have transparency before God, your relationship is so close that when pain and sickness come, you can cry out to him as your Abba Father.

Enter into "joy training" with God and prepare for whatever trial lies ahead.

Day 17

Joy and the Ending

Watching the Olympics is awesome, but don't you hate it when prime time coverage is pre-recorded?

Here's the solution. Avoid any news that day and you can pretend you're watching the Olympics live.

That's the way my wife likes it. As for me, I usually cheat and check the results ahead of time.

A few years ago, she got nervous watching the competition while I sat there calmly with a smirk on my face. She made me pledge that I wouldn't tell her the results.

I would head up to bed at the normal time and she'd watch until the very end.

I was calm because I knew the ending.

Someone told me the other day that we can have joy in this life, despite circumstances, because we know the end of the story. The Olympic analogy hardly compares to the reality of knowing the end as God reveals to us in Revelation, and this picture in chapter 19, verses 6-7 (NIV):

"Hallelujah!
   For our Lord God Almighty reigns.
Let us rejoice and be glad
   and give him glory!
For the wedding of the Lamb has come,
   and his bride has made herself ready."

And at the end of Revelation 17:14 (NIV), we who belong to

Christ enter into the picture:

"They will wage war against the Lamb, but the Lamb will triumph over them because he is Lord of lords and King of kings — and with him will be his called, chosen and faithful followers."

Let those passages sink in. Jesus will reign. We will reign with him in his Kingdom.

Our destination is heaven. If we die before he comes again, we'll be in his presence instantly when we leave this earth.

The journey in the here and now is full of trials and hardships. We can choose to let the hardships capture our senses. Or we can let our minds flash forward to the eternal victory we will experience — thanks to Jesus. Eternity with him!

The cares of this world will fade the more we focus on Jesus. Joy will be consistent, no matter what pain this world brings our way. It's not academic. It's real. It's deep.

When we meet Jesus, he will make us whole . . . body, mind, soul and spirit. Isn't that electrifying?

Stop and consider the ending. Reflect on it. It is nothing short of breathtaking. Read the entire chapter of Revelation 19. You'll erupt in joy!

Day 18

Joy and the Resurrection

The resurrection is the most joyful event in history.

Think about the contrast felt by Jesus' followers. He was crucified on Friday. The hopes that they had for their king to rule were dashed. They were banking on an earthly rule and being rescued from the oppression of Rome. Now their king was dead. Their expectations died with him.

The disciples scattered. Their faith vanished in a day. They didn't want to be caught as one of Jesus' followers. Three years of their lives were wasted following a dream. The foolish eleven shamefully faced going back to their jobs.

Then came Easter.

The two Marys were at the tomb and witnessed the supernatural:

"There was a violent earthquake, for an angel of the Lord came down from heaven and, going to the tomb, rolled back the stone and sat on it. His appearance was like lightning, and his clothes were white as snow." (Mathew 28:2 NIV)

If that wasn't astonishing enough, the angel spoke to the women:

"Do not be afraid, for I know that you are looking for Jesus, who was crucified. He is not here; he has risen, just as he said. Come and see the place where he lay. Then go quickly and tell his disciples: 'He has risen from the dead and is going ahead of you into Galilee. There you will see him.' Now I have told you." (Matthew 28:5-7 NIV)

The two Marys were the first to experience what all believers have experienced since then. Absolute . . . incomprehensible . . . outrageous . . . overflowing . . . JOY!

"So the women hurried away from the tomb, afraid yet filled with joy, and ran to tell his disciples." (Matthew 28:8 NIV)

They were *filled* with joy. Sorrow, depression and hopelessness were chased away by a God-given joy that reigned inside them.

How long has it been since you've taken time to consider the miracle of the resurrection? Not just a passing intellectual acknowledgment, but immersing yourself in the contrasting scenes: the crucifixion and the resurrection. You'll understand why the two Marys were filled with joy.

That same joy can flood your soul.

Pull out or click on your Bible. Slowly read through Matthew 27 and 28. View the stark contrast between the dashed hope of the crucifixion and the renewed hope of the resurrection.

Let God speak to you in this unhurried space. Allow your senses to go to those scenes two thousand years ago. Be wrapped up in the wonderful story of Jesus' resurrection.

Our joy rests in the truth that we, too, will be resurrected to be with Jesus. Forever. There is no greater blessing we can experience. It transcends any earthly pain we are suffering now.

May your joy be renewed today in such a way that every destructive thought or emotion is chased out of your life . . . just as they were chased out of the followers of Jesus two thousand years ago.

Day 19

Joy and the Word

Life happens and our joy is sucked right out of us. We're blindsided by getting fired, losing a good friend, receiving a call from our child's principal's office, or . . . you fill in the blank.

You might be in that place right now.

I understand.

I remember one of my most heart-wrenching moments. I heard about the death of a friend. He was only in his 30s and I learned the details on TV. The shock just killed me. I dropped to my knees in anguish before God and sobbed.

"No, no!" I shouted. "No, no!" Still, to this day, I grieve over the sudden loss of this dear friend.

How can our joy be restored when we are suddenly thrown to the depths?

The same way our joy is restored when we are lackluster, lukewarm or indifferent towards God and life.

I believe the Word of God is our anchor. There is something about his Word that feeds us supernaturally. Jesus said it himself, "It is written: 'Man shall not live on bread alone, but on every word that comes from the mouth of God.'" (Matthew 4:4 NIV)

Every single word of Scripture is from the mouth of God. We have a treasure trove of nourishment for our soul. This nourishment builds and restores joy. I can't explain how it happens, but it does.

How about the truth we camped on yesterday? *Jesus Christ rose from the dead.* "He is not here; he has risen, just as he said." (Matthew 28:6 NIV) Now that *really* makes me happy. Not the world's kind of happiness. *Joyful!* As only God can produce!

There are thousands of truths in the Bible that are foundational for our joy. I just mentioned one. Centering on that truth alone will drill deep into your soul and produce a consistent joy.

Whatever has robbed your joy, it's no match for God's Word. I encourage you to feed on God's Word today. Dwell on the truths that will build a deep joy in your life. A joy that will help you cope strongly with your current struggles.

Here are some promises you can read, think about and pray through.

God's inseparable love: "For I am convinced that neither death nor life, neither angels nor demons, neither the present nor the future, nor any powers, neither height nor depth, nor anything else in all creation, will be able to separate us from the love of God that is in Christ Jesus our Lord." (Romans 8:38-39 NIV)

The power of God's Word to change your life: "For the word of God is alive and active. Sharper than any double-edged sword, it penetrates even to dividing soul and spirit, joints and marrow; it judges the thoughts and attitudes of the heart." (Hebrews 4:12 NIV)

God relieves your fear: "So do not fear, for I am with you; do not be dismayed, for I am your God. I will strengthen you and help you; I will uphold you with my righteous right hand." (Isaiah 41:10 NIV)

Feed your soul with God's Word today. Feed joy.

Day 20

Joy and Your Thoughts I

What's on your mind these days?

I remember a lengthy season in my life when I was wrestling with some professional and personal issues that left me drained at the end of each day.

Over and over, I would play things through my mind. There was no resolution. I was plagued with the same thoughts day after day.

Have you ever had a season like that?

During those weeks, which stretched into months, I leaned into the Lord. I got more serious about immersing myself in his Word. I studied passages, even the entire book of Luke, in depth. I knew I had to wash myself with God's Word.

My prayer life became more intentional and regular. I often journaled my prayers to the Lord. I poured out my heart as I sought God's solution for my tough situation.

I can honestly say that despite the heartache, there was a sense of joy in my life. I could still face the day, laugh now and then and enjoy time with people. Despite everything pressing in on me, I had joy.

Yes, there was an underlying sense of angst. I won't kid you. But joy was still present.

I experienced what Nehemiah 8:10 (NIV) clearly states, "The joy of the Lord is your strength."

So I ask again, "What's on your mind these days?"

If joy escapes you because something is consuming your thoughts, I want to encourage you. Be intentional about your study of the Word and your attention to prayer.

If you're on top of the world right now and joy is filling your life, praise God! I still encourage you to go deep with God in the study of his Word and enjoy rich prayer times.

You see, it doesn't matter whether we're up or down, joyful or not, we need the food of the Word and oneness with God.

Meditate on this verse today. Use it as a trigger for your prayer time. Even now.

"Finally, brothers, whatever is true, whatever is honorable, whatever is just, whatever is pure, whatever is lovely, whatever is commendable, if there is any excellence, if there is anything worthy of praise, think about these things." (Philippians 4:8 ESV)

Day 21

Joy and Your Thoughts II

When we hear the word "meditation," we can easily reject the practice because it reminds us of Eastern mysticism.

It also means we have to slow down and be "unproductive" when there's so much to do. It means silence and that's tough in this world.

However, *Scriptural* meditation has enormous spiritual benefits.

If you want your joy to grow deep roots, think God's thoughts. Do that by meditating on his Word.

Why let Satan fill your mind with fear, jealousy, anger, greed, selfishness, impure thoughts and defeat? These things will rob your joy in an instant.

We can be blindsided by a sharp word from a friend, a financial emergency or a health issue.

Without a solid foundation, our joy will disintegrate.

How do you do Scriptural meditation and bring your thoughts in line with God's?

First, find a quiet time and place. That may be difficult in your world, but it's necessary if you want to go deep in the Word. Remove distractions, such as your phone, clutter and other things that steal your attention.

Second, choose a verse or passage of Scripture that speaks to you about something you're dealing with right now. At the end of today's devotion, I've listed some verses and passages that address common things that steal your joy.

Third, read the passage or verse several times. Let God bring certain parts of it alive to you. Spend time listening to the Lord and coming back to the passage.

Finally, see how much of the passage you can memorize. It could be a challenge for you, but try your best and ask the Lord for his help. You'll be internalizing God's Word, which brings lasting results as you battle against that thing you're dealing with right now.

As you go through the day, take the passage with you. Write it down and refer back to it. Read it when you have a few minutes. Continue to memorize it and let it penetrate your soul.

Meditating on God's Word will transform your thoughts and give you victory over the things that tear you down. As a result, joy will be a constant friend.

Here's what the Bible says about how to have victory over things that can steal your joy:

Fear: Isaiah 41:10 speaks of God's power over fear.
Jealousy: Ecclesiastes 4:4 gives perspective on how meaningless jealousy is.
Anger: James 1:19-20 instruct us in how to defeat anger.
Greed: I Timothy 6:8 teaches us about contentment.
Selfishness: Philippians 2:3 says humility is the solution.
Impure thoughts: Philippians 4:8 teaches us how to win the battle.
Conflict: Galatians 2:11 makes it clear how to deal with conflict.

Consider these verses and make them a part of your thought life.

Day 22

Joy in a Toxic Workplace

Are you in a workplace that robs your joy?

I was talking with a friend this morning who said that on Sunday afternoon he had a pit in his stomach thinking about work the next day.

He had started the day in worship with his family of believers. But, whatever joy he had experienced at church was wiped out with the thought of tomorrow.

Your work situation may not be that bad, but you may still sense a loss of joy almost daily.

You wrestle with that reality against a statement like this, "May the God of hope fill you with all joy and peace as you trust in Him." (Romans 15:13 NIV) And "Rejoice always, pray continually, give thanks in all circumstances." (I Thessalonians 5:16-17 NIV)

Reading those verses doesn't lift you up at all. Instead, you feel worse because you're failing to do what they say. You may even question your spiritual maturity.

A toxic work environment can bring down the strongest of believers.

It doesn't have to be that way with you. Consider this: You're not in your job by accident. God has chosen you to be there in his divine plan. That simple realization takes you out of your world into his.

Now imagine the possibilities! You're Christ's ambassador in your workplace.

I challenged my friend with one question. And I challenge you with the same one.

"What is *one* thing you can do to change the culture of your workplace?"

Whether you are in leadership or you're down the ladder, you can make a difference.

I'm not asking you to turn the company around. I'm asking you to consider the *one* thing you can do to change the culture in your sphere of influence.

Jesus changed the world one person at a time, one group of people at a time. He did some of his greatest work apart from large crowds. And his influence caught fire.

Your influence can catch fire, too. Not in your own power, but as the Holy Spirit uses you and He works in the hearts of people around you.

Start every day with the One Thing Challenge and watch joy re-enter your life.

Day 23

Joy Unlimited

"I will turn their mourning into gladness; I will give them comfort and joy instead of sorrow." (Jeremiah 31:13 NIV)

Notice the contrast that God uses in this verse. From the low of lows to the high of highs.

I like this verse because it challenges many Christians' belief that joy isn't an emotion. We've come to think that joy is an attitude of the heart while happiness is a temporary emotion.

However, look at the contrast here. Mourning and sorrow are emotions of deep sadness. God is using those words to put gladness and joy on display. The latter two are intense emotions. They are exhilarating.

When you're glad, you're smiling . . . laughing . . . happy! When you're joyful, your heart is bright and people can spot the vibrancy instantly. It's in your eyes, your smile, your actions. Yes, joy is an emotion to experience.

God offers you joy as a gift. He invites you to embrace it. More clearly, he invites you to open your heart and let him fill it with joy and gladness.

He says "*I* will turn their mourning into gladness; *I* will give them comfort and joy."

It's absurd to think that we can manufacture joy, but we sure try. It's short-lived.

The joy that God offers is a fruit of his Spirit. This is the furthest from manufactured joy. And it lasts!

"But the fruit of the Spirit is love, joy . . ." (Galatians 5:22 NIV)

God is waiting to reach deep into your heart and soul to flood you with his rich, genuine, long-lasting joy. He is the joy-giver.

What is your part in all this? Simply exhale and let God have your heart. No matter what state it's in.

This morning, a friend reminded me that exhaling spiritually is like emptying our lungs physically. It's relaxing. Try it now. It makes room for the joy God offers you as a gift.

As you practice this as a habit, you'll find that joy shows up more often, longer and more deeply in your life. It's God's supernatural joy. His gift to you.

Day 24

Lift Someone Up Today

"Therefore encourage one another and build each other up."
(I Thessalonians 5:11 NIV)

One of the best ways to experience joy is to get our eyes off ourselves.

We did an exercise at work recently that was downright encouraging. We were sitting at round tables with a sheet of paper in front of each of us. A co-worker's name was printed at the top. Our task was to write down one compliment about that person and then pass the paper along.

This exercise went on for 20 minutes as we wrote and passed, wrote and passed. A word, a phrase, a sentence for each person.

When we were finished, every sheet was filled with compliments. The leader then gave each person their sheet.

I read mine and I was instantly uplifted. No matter who you were in that room, no matter what your emotional state was when you walked in, you were feeling better when you left.

Two things happened that morning. Each person received encouragement reading their sheet of compliments, given by those they worked with every day.

I think a more important thing also happened. Each one of us was encouraged by giving compliments. We took our minds off ourselves for 20 minutes!

Self-centeredness can absolutely rob us of joy. We think we'll be happy by concentrating on our own needs. But the opposite happens.

Dwelling incessantly on personal struggles or being preoccupied with achieving great things lead to the same place. Isolation. And that's a joy killer for anyone.

Who comes to mind when you think of someone struggling right now?

A neighbor? Co-worker? Family member? A good friend?

Get that one person clearly pictured in your mind and answer these questions...

- What's their name?
- What's their struggle?
- How are they feeling right now?
- What is one thing you can do for them to lift them up?

Becoming the answer to that last question is your joy assignment today. It may simply be a phone call. It may be stopping by and praying for them. Or bringing a meal. It may be cleaning their house. Or sending them a card. For a co-worker, inviting them to lunch . . . and listening.

This person needs to know someone cares. They need someone to walk with them. They need encouragement.

Today, make someone's day. As a result, you'll be encouraged, too.

"Above all, keep loving one another earnestly, since love covers a multitude of sins. Show hospitality to one another without grumbling. As each has received a gift, use it to serve one another, as good stewards of God's varied grace." (I Peter 4:8-10 ESV)

Day 25

Practicing Joy I

A surgeon *practices* his profession. It doesn't mean he is rehearsing, experimenting with a few things here or there. That would be scary. A surgeon who is practicing is one who has completed his training and is now doing the real thing.

Contrast that with an athlete. He must practice over and over again so he will be fully prepared for competition.

We should practice joy like an athlete or musician, not like a surgeon. Again and again, doing what it takes to get better.

"Practicing joy?" you ask. "How hard can it be?"

It's a challenge to be joyful. Just observe your world as you go through the day today. At work, in the store, even at church. Count how many times you spot "joy." Not Joy the cashier, but "joy" the fruit of the Spirit.

How about joy in your own life? How much of your day yesterday was characterized by joy? Was it 20%, 50%, 70%? Off the top of your head, pick a number. Your first thought is probably the right number.

I believe we need to *practice* joy in order to experience it as a way of life. Not as a counterfeit, self-made joy, but one which is Christ-centered and Holy Spirit fed.

Today, let me suggest the first step to practicing joy. Tomorrow, we'll explore the second.

Hebrews 12:1 is our starting point, "Therefore, since we are surrounded by such a great cloud of witnesses, let us throw off everything that hinders and the sin that so easily entangles." (NIV)

You might be weighed down by heavy things. The stuff of life. What comes to mind when you think of the weights that hinder you? Write them down. Throw them off your mind and on to that piece of paper, phone, or tablet.

Then send an email to God with this short list of things that are weighing you down, hindering you. Yes, I know you'll get the email back. Just delete it. This exercise of releasing these things to God is the act of "throw(ing) off everything that hinders."

Next, throw off the sin that is entangling you. It's killing your joy. Confess it to God, claim the forgiveness of our Savior. Cast it to Jesus. You don't need to email this list to God — I don't recommend memorializing it.

These two simple acts will take just a few minutes. They will cleanse your heart, mind and soul. You'll be released from the things that hinder and entangle you.

The freedom and relief you'll feel will open the door to joy.

Let's talk about the next step tomorrow and what it really means to *practice* joy.

Enjoy your day of freedom today!

Day 26

Practicing Joy II

Yesterday, you went through the life-giving experience of Hebrews 12:1: "Let us throw off everything that hinders and the sin that so easily entangles." (NIV)

How did it feel? Like a burden lifted off your shoulders I hope. It should have made room for joy and other qualities of the fruit of the Spirit:

"Love, joy, peace, patience, kindness, goodness, faithfulness, gentleness, self-control." (Galatians 5:22-23 ESV)

But that was yesterday. Now here you sit today. Those burdens that hinder and sins that entangle are creeping back into your life.

I thought they were "thrown off" and cast to Jesus.

The truth is, life continues to come at us. The exercise of throwing off, casting away and confessing sin to Jesus is a daily exercise. That's what is means to *practice*. It's part of practicing joy.

Today, we consider together the second step of practicing joy. Together, these two steps can empower you and produce lasting joy in your life.

Here's step two, found again in Hebrews 12:1:

"And let us run with perseverance the race marked out for us." (NIV)

I think we can visualize "practice" better in this part of the verse. Imagine a long-distance runner. It takes practice, long hours of training, to build the stamina and muscle strength to run the race with perseverance.

Even short-distance runners practice their skills over and over again. Getting off the starting blocks, churning those legs, arm movements, head placement and much more.

Practicing joy is a race. A short-distance race today. A long-distance race for a lifetime.

You've thrown off those things that hinder you and you are free to run. What exactly does it mean to *run* when it comes to joy? What are you practicing?

Here are three exercises you can do in your training:

1. **Spend time enjoying God.** You've been freed up by throwing off your burdens and confessing your sin. There is an open line of communication between you and God. Enjoy the rich fellowship of prayer and reading through his Word. It's not complicated. Because you are right with God, your prayer life and Scripture reading will bring a newness that will fill your heart with joy.

2. **Thanksgiving.** Spend 10-15 minutes doing nothing but thanking God. Start by thanking your loving Father for the clean relationship you have with him and his Son Jesus. As you thank God for this, I won't be surprised if you're moved to tears. It is a wonderful thing to have a personal relationship with the God of the universe and his Son who died on the cross for you. From there, thank God for the blessings of your life. You might even find yourself thanking him for the difficult things. Strange but true.

3. **Tell others.** Share with family members or friends about the joy of God that you're experiencing. When it comes to joy, there's no way to keep it to yourself. You'll know a deeper joy just by sharing it.

That's what it means to practice joy. Of course, there are many other ways, but this coach has given you three.

Day 27

Praise and Joy

Throughout these pages, I hope you're learning that joy isn't something that you can produce yourself. You can't talk yourself into being joyful. That lasts about a day.

Joy is something that God forms inside you through his Holy Spirit. We can know it, but experiencing it is another thing.

Today, let's consider how praise is connected to our joy.

In fact, praise *leads* to joy and joy *leads* to praise.

They are siblings. Like two brothers who play well together for hours.

When I say praise, I'm referring to praising God for who He is. When you think through the character of God, and praise him for his character traits, your spirit will be lifted. Joy will emerge. Joy centered on the Father, Jesus and the Holy Spirit.

When you give God praise for who He is, there's no room for anything but Him.

God's *faithfulness* chases away doubt.

The Lord's *power* overcomes fear.

His Spirit's *holiness* pushes out sin.

Christ's *love* melts indifference.

The Father's *goodness* destroys our evil thoughts.

Here's an example of how your prayers centering on one attribute of God, his *faithfulness*, can completely transform your thoughts, spirit, emotions and soul:

Lord God, I praise you for your faithfulness. I can always count on you. You never leave me or forsake me. In my hardest times, you are there. In my happiest times, you laugh with me. When I sin and let you down, you stay with me. No matter what, you are faithful. I lift up my heart to you and honor you for your faithfulness. When people disappoint me, you don't.

Father, I look around me and see a world that seems out of control. But you are a faithful God who is ever-present and in control. You are true to your Word. Praise you for your faithfulness. I will never doubt you. Oh Lord, may I keep my eyes on you, the faithful Father that I know. What a blessing to know that I am a child of the faithful God. Amen and amen!

As you praise God for trait after trait, your heart will be filled with joy. Take your time and let the reality of each character quality sink in. Enjoy your time of praise, whether it be silent or aloud. God's Holy Spirit will give you a heart of joy.

That joy will lead to more praise. It's a wonderful cycle.

Set your alarm to pause at times during the day. Choose one attribute of God and get lost in praise.

Day 28

Joy and Shock

My wife and I were leaving town the next day and needed the doctor's report before we left. We had been waiting for almost a week for biopsy results. He had said it would only take two or three days.

We stood in the waiting room, knowing that the week-long wait was probably not a good sign. But I have to admit, we sensed God's peace through it all.

"Certainly, it's not cancer," we both thought. For my optimistic wife, that attitude was easy for her to come by. At first, I was certain the tests would come back negative. As the days slipped by, though, my confidence wavered.

We saw the doctor in the distance down the hall and kept our eyes focused on him when he approached us in the lobby. He seemed calm. He looked somewhat upbeat. He smiled and asked us to come back with him to one of the offices.

We followed him as he looked for an empty room. We entered and he quietly closed the door.

He turned to us. We were all still standing there. The only words I remember him saying were, "It's bad."

He went on to tell us that my wife had cancer. He explained that it had fooled the analysts in three different labs until one finally verified the type of cancer.

So how do you respond in a situation like this? I was disoriented, but remarkably at peace. I can't explain it.

Noonie was steady. She, too, was at peace. She has her own story of this journey through cancer that she often shares with others.

But, for that moment, time seemed to stand still. We didn't know what questions to ask or even what the next step would be. We were new at this and were about to walk down a well-travelled road that we had never before set foot on.

Yes, we had peace. How about joy?

I can't speak for Noonie, but for me, it was gone in an instant. Or had it been slipping away all week?

James writes, "Count it all joy, my brothers, when you meet trials of many kinds." (James 1:2 ESV)

You might be caught in a shocking situation like ours, where joy has been sucked out of your life. You've been hit with a painful blow.

Horrible health news. A job loss. A severed relationship. A child walking away from you or the Lord. Losing a loved one or a good friend.

If this describes you right now, there is no formula for bringing joy back into your life. God is not a formulaic God. He is a person who loves and indwells you if you know his Son Jesus.

Joy comes from the inside out as you draw on your relationship with God. Totally immerse yourself in him. Recapturing joy will be as unique to you as it was for Noonie and me after that bad news day. It's your personal journey.

Today, give yourself time to retreat with God. Clear out time . . . 15 minutes, 30 minutes, however long you need. Retreat to a quiet place. Just you and the Lord.

Share with Jesus your pain, grief, confusion, shock. Cry out to him. The Holy Spirt will begin a work of "joy restoration" in you.

Day 29

Spreading Joy

Look around today at people you encounter. Notice how many of them have looks of pain, indifference and emptiness. We live in a world that often saps the life out of us.

When Christ is at the center of our lives and we are filled with the joy of the Holy Spirit, we stand out. We're strange, in fact, in a good way.

In the early verses in John 15, Jesus speaks to us about abiding in him as a branch abides in the vine. The life-giving resources of Jesus flow into us.

"As the branch cannot bear fruit by itself, unless it abides in the vine, neither can you, unless you abide in me. I am the vine; you are the branches. Whoever abides in me and I in him, he it is that bears much fruit." (John 15:4-5 ESV)

Jesus culminates this illustration in verse 11, "These things I have spoken to you, that my joy may be in you, and that your joy may be full."

He promised "that *my* joy may be in you."

You have the joy of the living Savior inside you. It's a supernatural joy that transcends circumstances, feelings, difficult relationships and even your own sin.

He also promised "that your joy may be *full*."

When I think of the word "full," I think of overflowing. When our joy is overflowing, it's contagious. We spread it to others.

I'm not sure where your joy meter is today, but you have the opportunity to be a blessing to the people around you. For the glory of God.

Perhaps you're running low on joy and you don't have much to share with others.

Joy doesn't just happen. We need to immerse ourselves in Jesus. It comes back to spending time with him and in the Word of God.

For you right now, it may mean starting with John 15. Read through it and let God make "abiding" real in your life today. You aren't supposed to grow joy in your life. It's fruit that the Holy Spirit produces in you as you abide in Christ.

Let's face it. If we're full of joy, we can't help but to show it and spread it around. It's in our attitude, words, actions and emotions.

A friend may ask you, "Why are you so happy today?" You can tell them the reason for your joy.

Today, consider how you can spread the joy of Jesus. You could change someone's day.

Day 30

Your Joy Network

There's a quote going around these days that says, "You are the average of the five people you spend the most time with."

I don't know if Jim Rohn's statement is a proven fact, but it sure makes sense.

When it comes to your walk with God, who do you hang out with?

More specifically, when it comes to your walk with God, do you have a joy network?

How in the world can we expect to have a heart of joy if we're going it alone? Sure, we can be hanging out with solid believers, but these believers may not be joyful. Find ones who are!

God created us to *need* people. The Bible is written not to individuals, but to communities of believers . . . the church.

"If one part suffers, every part suffers with it; if one part is honored, every part rejoices with it. Now you are the body of Christ, and each of you is a member of it." (I Corinthians 12:26-27 NIV)

If you are to do life with other believers, it makes sense that your closest friends are ones who have hearts of joy. You see, the faith of these believers is likely rooted deeply in Christ. He is the one who gives joy. It's a fruit of the Spirit.

Am I saying to stay away from people who are Eeyore's? No, you can have a powerful ministry in their lives. But don't surround yourself with them. They'll pull you down.

Surround yourself with people of joy. A Joy Network!

Off the top of your head, name a handful of Christian friends whose lives are characterized by joy. When you think of them, you smile. The word "joy" is attached to them.

Today, pray for each one of them. Just a short prayer, even now, that God will use them to bring joy to the lives of others.

Secondly, seek them out. Hang out with them. Pray with them. Laugh with them. Find out why they are joyful. Bring joy to their lives.

Form your own Joy Network of 4-5 friends that will empower you with joy so you can be an ambassador of God's joy to others.

**Continue your journey with God.
Start the next devotional in the series.**

30 Days of Faith

Day 1: Finding Faith

After an experience that would change my destiny, I walked through the front door and stood in our living room. An hour earlier, I had heard the Gospel for the first time at a tiny church in Upstate New York. Seated on the couch, my parents asked me how the meeting went. I blurted out, "I was born again!" You should have seen the puzzled looks on their faces.

I hardly knew what it meant to be born again, but that's how my journey of faith began nearly five decades ago as a high school junior.

I had gone to the church service on a cold, snowy January night to hear a college football coach speak. However, he didn't talk about football. I was tricked! He told the story of a man from the Bible named Nicodemus. This ruler of the Jews approached Jesus in the darkness of night with a hunger to know God.

Jesus explained to Nicodemus that he needed a spiritual birth to know God. He had to be born again. I felt like Nicodemus, because no one had ever told me this.

I'll never forget one part of the coach's message. He told us that whenever he was on a flight, he'd say to the person next to him, "If this plane were to go down tonight, do you know where you'd spend eternity?" How's that for a conversation-starter?

That night, I put my faith in Jesus for my salvation.

Your faith journey to Christ might be more dramatic than mine was as a 16-year-old. On the other hand, maybe you grew up in a Christian home and you can't point to the exact moment you put your faith in Jesus. We all own a unique faith journey, each one as valid as the next.

Perhaps you're that person, like Nicodemus, who is searching for God. You're on a stealth expedition, as Nicodemus was in the darkness with Jesus. I encourage you to read his story in John 3.

Your faith journey continues as we walk together for the next 30 days. Whether you'd describe your faith as strong or weak, it's healthy to look back on that time when you exercised your biggest step of faith: believing Jesus for your eternal destiny. There's no greater faith step than that. It's a big deal.

Celebrate. Rejoice in your salvation! Recall your story, just as I have. Think about the details. What did you feel? Who else was there? Replay the scene in your mind. Relive it. You might want to tell your story over a meal to experience it with your family.

Have fun reflecting on your journey. Think about when you first understood that Jesus died for your sins and you put your faith in him. It was the starting point of your new life in Christ. Paul affirms, "Therefore, if anyone is in Christ, he is a new creation. The old has passed away; behold, the new has come." (2 Corinthians 5:17 ESV)

Your faith journey will always have its ups and downs. That's why it's good to look back on your first step of faith and remember your roots. Your destiny was changed for eternity.

Day 2: Faith Heroes

Have you ever wished you could have the faith of Paul? Moses? Noah? Or some other Bible great?

It's only natural to compare ourselves to someone else, even when it comes to our spiritual life. That someone today may be one of your Christian friends. Or it could be a person you've never met but you've put on a pedestal.

My faith hero was Dr. Bill Bright, founder of Campus Crusade for Christ. Later in this devotional, you'll find out why.

While it's good to look up to someone, remember this: No one else has your story.

Your story of faith is one that God is writing, full of twists and turns.

Paul's story was dramatic, difficult and daring.

Moses' story was lonely, long and liberating.

Noah's story was challenging, chilling and charged.

What three words describe your faith story?

For me, they would be pioneering, prayerful and periodic. They describe phases of my life with God.

My wife's faith story would probably have a "c" in it. Cancer. It was an extremely difficult season for her, but it was a year of spiritual growth and life lessons. God became more real to her than at any other time in her life.

Think for a few minutes about three words that sum up your walk of faith. They don't have to start with the same letter.

1. _____

2. _____

3. _____

Once you have those three words, reflect on why you chose them. Think about the seasons of life those words describe. How do they make you feel? Where do you see God in the midst?

You're reflecting on the unique story God is writing. It's your faith story. Like those of the Bible greats, it isn't all wonderful. That's ok. It's not over.

God has given you a story to tell. It's a story that will bring glory to him as you tell others. God is in the midst of your story and others need to hear that. You'll encourage them in their faith story and you may lead them to Jesus for the first time.

As a result, your own faith will grow.

Day 3: Faith and Children

Our home has several crawl spaces that are accessible on the second floor. Small doors open to a secret world kids love to explore. As adults, we know these spaces as the attic.

Our grandchildren are ready to crawl and walk through this secret world without reservation. In fact, one of our grandsons said, "Grandpa, you live in a castle!"

As for me, I enter these spaces cautiously. For some reason, I don't trust the plywood and massive joists to hold me up. I envision falling through to the floor below. My fear is unfounded, but real.

All my grandchildren are less fearful that I am! They'll play in the attic with no reservation at all while I'm afraid to go in. How's that for being humbled?

In my walk with God, I wish I had the faith of a five-year-old. A five-year-old believes, no questions asked.

The same "attic fear" creeps into my life. I'm sure you have some of that, too. These might be some of your fearful thoughts . . .

"Lord, are we going to be able to pay our bills?"

"God, my kids are turning away from you."

"Father, please make this pain be nothing serious."

Our God is trustworthy. We know that. So why do we doubt God when the stuff of life hits? Why is our faith shaky?

How can I have the faith of a five-year-old?

I think the solution is to know God for who he is. That may sound simple . . . because it is.

We have a habit of making God in *our* image. We won't openly admit it, but we think God is limited.

Here's who God really is.

Eternal. "I am the Alpha and the Omega," says the Lord God, "who is, and who was, and who is to come, the Almighty." (Revelation 1:8 NIV)

Trustworthy and faithful. "God has said, 'Never will I leave you; never will I forsake you.'" (Hebrews 13:5 NIV)

Giver of everlasting life. "Jesus said to her, 'I am the resurrection and the life. The one who believes in me will live, even though they die.'" (John 11:25 NIV)

Powerful. "For who is God besides the Lord? And who is the Rock except our God?" (2 Samuel 22:32 NIV)

Lord of all. "He determines the number of the stars and calls them each by name. Great is our Lord and mighty in power; his understanding has no limit." (Psalm 147:4-5 NIV)

Love and loving. "So we have come to know and to believe the love that God has for us. God is love." (I John 4:16 ESV)

Good. "For you, O Lord, are good and forgiving, abounding in steadfast love to all who call upon you." (Psalm 86:5 ESV)

This is the God who is at the center of our faith. It's dangerous when we wander away from these truths and see God as weak, incapable, finite and not worthy of our trust. How tragic.

Immerse yourself in the true God. Study the verses above. Think about them. Let the reality of who God is sink in. He is the one you can always turn to.

Experience the rest of this devotional.

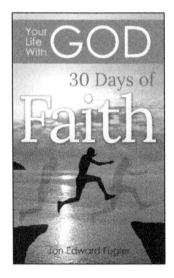

Buy it on Amazon.

Also for your journey:

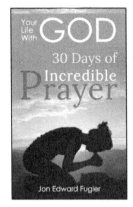 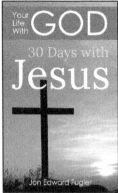 

Available on Amazon.

About the Author

Jon Edward Fugler

 Assembling sentences goes way back for Jon Edward Fugler. Growing up in Upstate New York, his first writing effort was to publish a neighborhood newspaper — which lasted one issue. In middle school, he printed and distributed a newsletter to his classmates and teachers reporting on his board game baseball league.

In 1973, Jon came to know Christ after hearing a college football coach speak about how to be born again. This event would change the course of his life and writing.

He spent over 30 years in Christian radio, turning out script after script, beginning as the radio writer for Dr. Bill Bright, founder of Campus Crusade for Christ. From there, he wrote scores of scripts that would impact the hearts of radio listeners across the country.

Journaling has been Jon's habit for over four decades. He sometimes looks back on those writings to inspire him for his current works. His conversational style connects with readers on a personal level. Writing from his heart, he hopes readers' lives will be different through their relationship with Jesus Christ.

"It's not about performing for Jesus," says Jon. "It's about living with Jesus."

He was influenced by author Skye Jethani, who teaches that life over, under, from or for God leads to defeat. Life *with* God is what every person desires. Jon sensed that developing a *habit* of experiencing life *with* God was missing for believers. That's what inspired him to write his devotional series, starting with **Your Life with God: 30 Days of Joy**.

"I feel that if someone can immerse themselves in one aspect of the Christian life for 30 days, it will change them," says Jon. "This series is not about behavior. It's all about relationship. The reader's relationship with God. Growth happens when a person lets God flood their life."

Jon's passion is that every person on earth has access to the gospel. He is active today in ministry taking the Good News to the world. He and his wife live in North Carolina. They have three children and seven grandchildren.

Jon wants to know how this 30-day experience with joy has affected your life. Share your joy story with Jon at jon@yourlifewithgod.com.

If you enjoyed this devotional, please leave a review at www.yourlifewithgod.com/review.

The Devotional Series

Our walk with God is a relationship, not a performance. Yet, we often get trapped in performance Christianity, which leads to a dead end. Frustrated, we try to climb out.

However, we tend to revert back to *doing* the right things for God. Frustration returns. The cycle continues.

In his devotional series, *Your Life With God*, Jon Edward Fugler leads you into a fresh relationship with the Lord. He helps you break the cycle of performance through a 30-day experience immersed in a single aspect of the Christian life.

By spending a few minutes each day, you'll be nurtured and refreshed. You'll have a new perspective on your relationship with Jesus. This will translate into your moment-by-moment life with God.

There's more on the way . . .

Be sure to get advance notice when the next devotional comes out by signing up on Jon's **VIP Readers** list on the series website:

www.YourLifeWithGod.com

Made in the USA
Monee, IL
21 November 2020